A HERO
AND THE
HOLOCAUST
The Story of Janusz Korczak
and His Children

BY DAVID A. ADLER

ILLUSTRATED BY
BILL FARNSWORTH

Holiday House / NEW YORK

Library of Congress Cataloging-in-Publication Data
Adler, David A.
A Hero and the Holocaust: The story of Janusz Korczak and His Children /
David A. Adler; illustrated by Bill Farnsworth.—1st ed.
p.   cm.
Summary: A brief biography of the Polish doctor, author,
founder of orphanages, and promoter of children's rights,
who lost his life trying to protect his orphans
from the Nazis.
ISBN 0-8234-1548-1 (hardcover)
1. Korczak, Janusz, 1878–1942—Juvenile literature.
2. Jewish educators—Poland—Warsaw—
Biography—Juvenile literature. 3. Holocaust, Jewish (1939–1945)—
Poland—Warsaw—Juvenile literature. 4. Warsaw (Poland)—
Biography—Juvenile literature.
[1. Korczak, Janusz, 1878–1942. 2. Jews—Poland—
Biography. 3. Educators. 4. Jews—Persecutions—
Poland—Warsaw.
5. Holocaust, Jewish (1939–1945)—
Poland—Warsaw.]
I. Farnsworth, Bill, ill. II. Title.

LB775.K6272 A43 2002
943.8'4—dc21   2001059409

In memory of an estimated 1.5 million children,
victims of the Holocaust
D. A. A.

To my wife Deborah and my daughters,
Allison and Caitlin
B. F.

IN EUROPE, 1878 WAS A YEAR OF GREAT PROMISE.

In Rome, a new pope was chosen. A new king was crowned.

In Paris, there was an international exhibit, the largest ever up to that time, with thousands of displays. Among them was a statue "representing liberty enlightening the world." After the fair, this *Statue of Liberty* was sent to the United States, a gift of the French people.

But in 1878, there was a hint, too, of coming tragedy. In Gotha, Germany, Europe's first crematorium was built for use at funerals.

Janusz Korczak was born in 1878, in Warsaw. He would become one of Poland's leading citizens, a hero during Europe's darkest hours.

When Korczak was young, Warsaw was still beautiful. It was built on the banks of the Vistula River, with cobblestone streets, chestnut trees, public gardens, several palaces, and even a royal castle.

Korczak's parents were Jozef and Cecylia Goldszmit, a successful lawyer and the daughter of an important businessman. They were Jewish, but not religious people. They named their son after his grandfather, but instead of the Jewish-sounding Hirsh, they called him Henryk. The name Janusz Korczak would come later.

Young Henryk Goldszmit was a quiet child. He played with his blocks for hours and daydreamed. His dreams, he said, were like "telling myself fairy tales." Later, when Henryk discovered books, he lost himself in them.

Henryk had friends, too, and often walked to nearby Saski Park, where, he later wrote, "I talked to people a lot, to peers and to much older grown-ups... I had some really aged friends. They admired me. A philosopher, they said."

Suddenly, in 1889, Henryk's quiet life changed forever. His father had a mental breakdown. He was hospitalized and died in 1896, at the age of fifty-two. Henryk mourned his father and feared that one day he, too, might go mad.

After Jozef Goldszmit's death, the family was impoverished. They sold their fancy furniture, fine paintings, and good dishes. Henryk worked after school. He tutored children. His mother took in boarders.

Henryk also began to write sad stories and poems.

"Ah, let me die," he wrote. "Let me fall into my dark grave."

He wrote a play about a madman and his family and submitted it to a contest. He took a pen name for the contest, Janusz Korczak, perhaps so the judges wouldn't know he was Jewish. The play won an honorable mention.

He continued to use that pen name, and to most people Henryk Goldszmit was known as Janusz Korczak.

Korczak studied medicine at the University of Warsaw. When he graduated, he worked in a children's hospital. "I always felt best among children," he said.

He wrote stories for children and books of advice for adults. He told adults to respect children and their beliefs, and most of all, to love them.

Janusz Korczak became the director of a new Jewish orphans' home. He gave out candies there, told stories and jokes, and did magic tricks. He gave children crayons and told them to draw on his bald head. He helped them with their homework and joined in their games.

The children loved him.

When Korczak sat outside, young children climbed over him, played with his goatee, and often fell asleep in his lap. He just smiled. "I look like an old tree," he said, and the children are "like birds in my branches."

At the orphans' home, Korczak was his children's doctor, barber, teacher, and father. He clipped their nails, cut their hair, and fixed their shoes. For each baby tooth that fell out, he paid a "reward." Then he used the teeth to build a toy castle.

In the evenings, Korczak and his helpmate Stefania Wilczyska went from bed to bed, talked to the children, tucked them in, and wished them a good night.

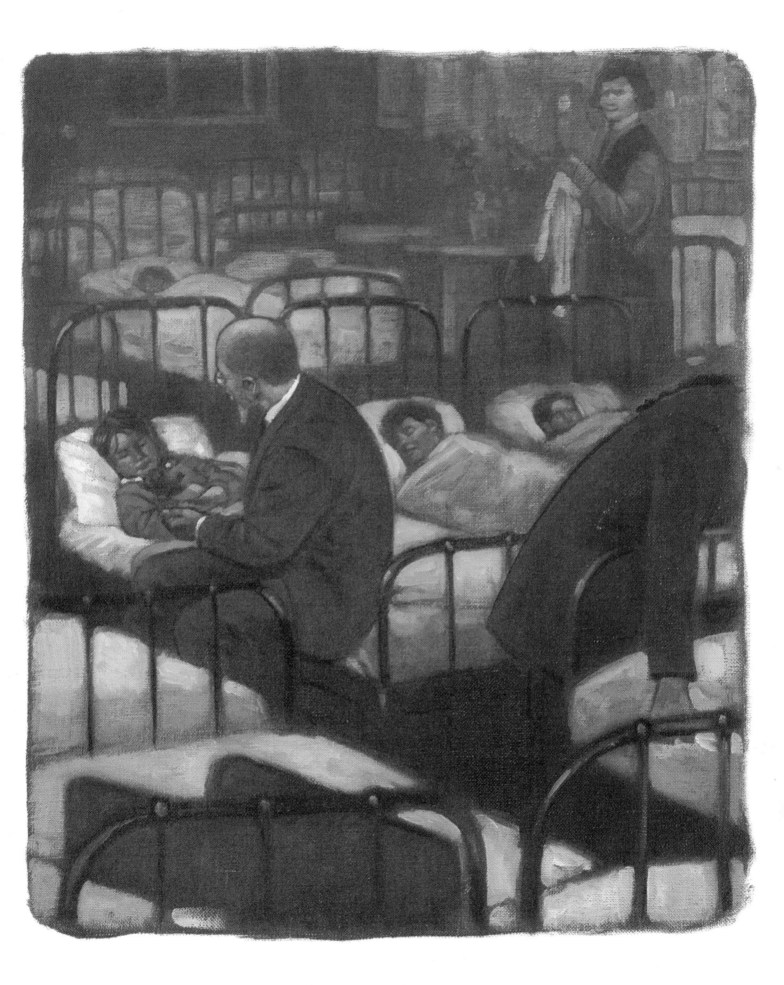

In the 1930s, when radio was new and exciting, Korczak had a weekly program of stories and advice.

Korczak's books and radio programs were famous. Janusz Korczak was awarded the Golden Laurel by the Polish Academy of Literature and the Silver Cross by the Polish Republic for his contributions to the nation.

The 1930s were a grim time for Europe. In 1933, in Berlin, 350 miles from Warsaw, the anti-Jewish Nazi Party took control of Germany. Books were burned. Property was seized.

In 1938, German troops marched into Austria.

Beginning on Friday, September 1, 1939, German forces attacked Warsaw and other cities in Poland. There were days when the shooting and bombing went on without stop. By the end of September, Poland fell.

Nazis followed German troops into Poland. They attacked Jews in the street, stole their property and businesses, and sent them to forced labor camps. They forced each Jew to wear a Star of David armband.

Janusz Korczak declared, "I can promise you I will never wear an armband!"

In 1940, he was arrested and jailed for not obeying Nazi law. After a month, he was released. But a year later, he was arrested again. This time, a friend helped free him.

Beginning in April 1940, an eight-foot-high wall topped with barbed wire was built in Warsaw. It enclosed seventy-three streets. More than four hundred thousand Jews, including Korczak and his children, were forced to live inside those walls, in the Warsaw Ghetto.

Korczak did not want moving into the ghetto to frighten his children, so he led them in a "kind of parade." At the very front were Korczak and a child holding the green flag of King Matt, the child-king hero of one of Korczak's stories. The children sang as they marched to their new home in the ghetto.

In 1941, the Nazis reduced the size of the ghetto and the children had to move again.

In January 1940, Korczak began a diary but made only a few entries. Then, beginning in May 1942, he wrote more regularly. He described the ghetto as "a plague-stricken area… a lunatic asylum." He called it "a prison."

Several families were crowded into each apartment. There was never enough food, never enough coal and wood to burn for heat, never enough medicine. There were thousands of beggars. People stood with their few possessions, hoping to trade something for a piece of bread. Thousands of people in the ghetto died each month from starvation and disease.

Korczak wrote, "The children are living in constant uncertainty, in fear."

On July 22, 1942, signs were posted. The ghetto would be emptied. Jews would be taken east, to work. But people knew this was a lie. They would be taken to a Nazi death camp, and killed. Their remains would be destroyed in a crematorium. On August 4, Korczak wrote in his diary. "A cloudy morning. Five-thirty. Seemingly an ordinary beginning of a day." He also wrote that day of his children's smiles. "They are ill, pale, lung-sick smiles."

Two days later, on August 6, the Nazis came for Korczak's orphans.

Korczak was given fifteen minutes to get ready. He told his children they need not be afraid. No matter what happened, he would be with them. He told them to each find something to take along, perhaps a toy or a favorite book. Then they lined up outside, two by two. They followed their beloved "Old Doctor" and the green flag of King Matt.

Korczak, his helpers, and 192 children looked straight ahead and sang a marching song as they walked two miles to the train station. They passed a Jewish graveyard, with bodies piled high, not yet buried. They followed Janusz Korczak.

There were reports that at the very last moment a Nazi commander recognized the famous Korczak and offered to let him go free. But Janusz Korczak refused to leave his children.

People cried, screamed, begged not to be forced onto the trains. But Korczak calmly helped his children aboard.

The train took them northeast about sixty miles, to
Treblinka. At the station, there were fake fronts of a
restaurant, barbershop, and bakery. There were signs for
trains to other cities. But for Jews, there were no trains
out of Treblinka.

Janusz Korczak died there with his children.
Among his last diary entries, Korczak wrote, "I never
wish anyone ill. I cannot. I don't know how it is done."

AUTHOR'S NOTE

While the year of Janusz Korczak's birth is often given as 1878, it is not certain. In 1942, he wrote in his diary, "Tomorrow I shall be sixty-three or sixty-four years old. For some years, my father failed to obtain my birth certificate. I suffered a few difficult moments over that."

When he was a child, Korczak's mother used to watch him play quietly and said he had no ambition. His father called him a "clod, fool, and idiot." But his grandmother called him "little philosopher."

Korczak served as a doctor in the army during three wars, the Russo-Japanese War, First World War, and Polish-Soviet War.

Korczak took the name "The Old Doctor" for his radio programs because officials at the radio station didn't want it known that they were broadcasting a Jew's advice to the general public.

SELECTED BIBLIOGRAPHY

Adler, Stanislaw. *In the Warsaw Ghetto, 1940–1943: An Account of a Witness, The Memoir of Stanislaw Adler,* translated by Sara Chmielewska Philip. Jerusalem: Yad Vashem, 1982.

Bernheim, Mark. *Father of the Orphans: The Story of Janusz Korczak.* New York: Lodestar/Dutton, 1989.

Encyclopedia Britannica, Eleventh Edition. New York: The Encyclopedia Britannica Company, 1911.

Kermish, Joseph, editor. *To Live With Honor And Die With Honor!: Selected Documents from the Warsaw Ghetto Underground Archives, "O.S." ("Oneg Shabbath").* Jerusalem: Yad Vashem, 1986.

Korczak, Janusz. *Ghetto Diary,* translated by Jerzy Bachrach and Barbara Krzywicka. New York: Holocaust Library, 1978.

—— *King Matt the First,* translated by Richard Lourie. New York: Farrar, Straus & Giroux, 1986.

Ringelblum, Emanuel. *Notes from the Warsaw Ghetto: The Journal of Emanuel Ringelblum,* edited and translated by Jacob Stern. New York: McGraw-Hill, 1958.